EARTH GIANT TREE GIFT SERIES – BOOK 4

Rainbow Gum's Gift

ROCHELLE HEVEREN

TREE VOICE PUBLISHING
www.treevoice.global

Earth Giant Tree Gift Series: Rainbow Gum's Gift

TREE VOICE PUBLISHING PTY LTD
ACN. 627 784 294 ABN . 94627784294
4 Wirreanda Court Blackbun Victoria 3130 AUSTRALIA
Phone +613 9878 4600
Email: hello@treevoice.global
www.treevoice.global

First published in 2018
Copyright text © Rochelle Heveren
Copyright © Tree Voice Publishing

business.facebook.com/TreeVoiceAuthor
www.facebook.com/RochelleHeverenAuthor
Instagram: @rochelle_with_love_x

All rights reserved. No part of this publication may be reproduced in whole or in part, stored in a retrievable system, or transmitted in any form or by any means, electronic, mechanical, photocopying, recording or otherwise, without written permission of the copyright holder or publisher.

Designed by Tree Voice Publishing Pty Ltd
Printed by Ingram Spark
ISBN: 978-0-6483521-3-6 (paperback)

A catalogue record for this book is available from the National Library of Australia

Praise for 'Rainbow Gum's Gift'

"I was so blown away reading how Rochelle was able to free herself from her painful past by connecting with the beautiful rainbow gum tree. The lessons she gleaned from this spiritual connection are applicable for anyone seeking joy – a beautiful story."

Megan Castran
Jewelchic

"Reading about Rochelle's experience meeting Rainbow Gum was uplifting. I had tears whilst also feeling great joy. I felt I could reach out and hug Rainbow Gum. I had an experience of great joy and deep emotion when I hand delivered something for Rochelle, having lost my own mother one year ago.

This book reminds every kind heart to be open and full to all the love and joy that life has to offer. Thank you Rochelle for sharing with everyone the joy of the Rainbow Gum."

Una Grimes
Eltham Victoria

"I felt extremely honoured to read the beautiful 'Rainbow Gum's Gift'. I instantly connected to the joy that I also felt at her base when I was in Maui Hawaii. This book is full of love and wisdom which I am grateful to be uplifted by. Thank you Rochelle for sharing."

Tracey Hudson
Neerim South Victoria

"'Rainbow Gum's Gift' is a beautiful simple enjoyable read and yet so profound for all who are searching for answers to their life journey questions. As you quickly emerge into the story you find hidden wisdom and treasures that can help you find inner awareness to improve your life journey.

Rochelle has brought awareness and understanding back to the centre point of what life is about, the ability to find heart centred love. She has captured the value of what nature can teach in the responses given by the Rainbow Gum to her probing questions. Thank you for an enjoyable experience."

Karl Camden-Burch
Intuitive Life Coach

Foreword

Rainbow Gum's Gift is the channelled teachings of one of Earth's great Sisters. The wise Eighty-year-old Rainbow Gum brings you freedom from all past pains and hurts, self-love and a unique way of guiding life's journey.

She'll remind you of the importance of living through your heart, your connection of love to others, gifts and the importance of being present. She'll guide you through the challenges of feeling stuck in the past, frustrated by habit, lonely and full of sadness. She will help open your heart and mind to untold possibilities and assist you to live your highest truth with compassion, stillness and joy beyond anything you ever dreamed.

Being supported with the magic of *Rainbow Gum's Gift* is like resting your back on the vibrant trunk and listening to her whispers of great wisdom. Allow her words to caress you and fill you with love.

This inspiring gift book is designed to unlock your own hearts wisdom. Rochelle invites you to discover the magic, love, feeling free of all past hurt and pain and joy that she experienced, sitting and resting her back against the Rainbow Gum.

Written in Maui, Hawaii

Contents

Introduction 1

Chapter 1: Rainbows 2

Chapter 2: Choice 10

Chapter 3: A Shift in Being 13

Chapter 4: Between Opposites 16

Chapter 5: Rainbow's Beginning 19

Chapter 6: Freedom 23

Chapter 7: Simple Pleasures 25

Chapter 8: Held by Angel 31

Chapter 9: Love is a Gift 34

Chapter 10: I Am 39

Chapter 11: Happy Birthday 43

Introduction

Whenever a storm breaks open the sky, the thrashing rain pours down from the heavens, falling down on me. If I stand for too long in the downpour, eventually I too fall to the ground.

The pain and hurts of yesterday had still left me feeling like I was standing in a rainstorm.

I never imagined the impact that connecting with Rainbow Gum would have on my life. It stopped the rains and settled the storms of my past. The sun finally shone over my existence. A rainbow of promise stretched across my life sky.

My time connecting to Rainbow with an open heart was one of the most profound shifts in my existence.

At first I wasn't sure if I should share Rainbow Gum's gift. Then I knew I couldn't keep it from others.

Wishing 'Joy' to all.

CHAPTER 1

Rainbows

When friends invite us to travel to Hawaii to meet them, I am instantly excited. Michael and I have been married for over 28 years and it was to Maui, Hawaii that we first travelled as husband and wife, on our honeymoon.

My bag is full, as well as my heart.

Maui is so beautiful.

Our accommodation is perfect. The room looks out over the many plunge pools, and onto long patches of lush, green grass that connect to the sandy coastline. Palm trees beautifully complete the tropical scene. Our first evening is warm as the sun sets gracefully, casting a pink and blue hue across the sky. Michael and I take a stroll, hand in hand, along the beach to watch the stunning setting sun. I am enveloped in Michael's love.

I have always loved the feeling and smell of fresh sheets. The white linen in our resort bed is perfect. Crossing an international time zone, we have lost a day and I am exhausted. As Michael holds me, I settle to sleep. This feels special.

The next day we explore Maui. On our first lap around the southern section of the island, I am excited when I spot a heap of incredible rainbow gums on the roadside.

It begins to rain but there is nowhere to pull the car over. Michael promises that we will return to explore this area another time. The road to Hana is an adventure, and Michael loves driving along the winding trail. The road zigzags around and above sheer cliff faces. We look down on the ocean as it crashes onto the shoreline below. We stop at a ranch-style road house and devour big barbeque burgers. Back on the road the landscape changes from steep mountains to sprawling countryside, scattered with volcanic rock, once an erupted volcano that covered most of Maui. For much of the day it continues to rain. It reminds us of our honeymoon all those years ago.

In the late afternoon we spot signage back towards the coast, back to where we saw the beautiful rainbow gum trees earlier. We take a right turn and this time we can pull over. Surprisingly, we have the area all to ourselves.

Jumping out of the car I put up my umbrella, trying to also cover Michael. The track is a running stream and the ground is very muddy. We are taken up to the grove of rainbow gums. There are many trees here. The rain is heavy but somehow we barely notice it as we are both captivated by the beauty of the trunks and branches of the many trees. They are all magically striped with the many colours of the rainbow.

Michael forges ahead while I take my time, trying to ensure I don't slip. I hear him calling to me to catch up. He is standing in front of the largest Rainbow Gum at the back of the group by the road. He smiles and tells me that he has found the most beautiful tree – he had found the mother of this grove.

I am instantly struck by the grace and poise of the most vibrant tree I have ever seen. We are both excited.

The rain becomes heavier, if that is possible, and like a river it runs down Rainbow's trunk. I cup and drink some of the water – it is sweet. From every angle I take photos. Walking around Rainbow's trunk

I see intricate details and markings of bark strips highlighted by the manifold colours of the rainbow.

Michael leaves me alone with my new friend.

I take three breaths into my heart, stilling my mind and opening a space where both Rainbow and I can connect.

"Hello," I say, "You are beautiful. I feel instantly happy standing here by you."

"Stand and inhale my air, feel and experience joy," Rainbow says softly.

That is exactly how I feel. I am full of joy. I have worked really hard on capturing this very emotion all my life – and here I am standing in the presence of joy itself.

"Stand with your back against me."

Doing so, I feel instant alignment. Energy races up my spine and out through my instant calm, clear mind.

"Thank you," I whisper, in no hurry to break the magical spell. "Do many people visit you here on the roadside heading towards Hana? Does everyone become re-aligned in your presence?"

"Everyone is open to the magic. It takes surrender to stand and trust," Rainbow replies.

I continue to stand with my feet firmly squished into the muddy earth beneath and around Rainbow. Even though the rain has soaked me through, I am in no hurry to leave.

This Rainbow Gum is special. Planted back from the main row of gums that line the road, she has plenty of space around her. When I glance down, I notice that her big root system connects all of this grove together. I think about the support they must give each other.

"I have noticed at my farm, the gums are like a family living together. Are the other Rainbow Gums here part of your family?" I ask.

"Gums are always part of a community, a family. We are connected. You will never see just one gum."

"You are the mother here, aren't you?" I ask to check if my hunch is correct.

"Yes, I am."

Threading heart to heart I feel her history seeping within my being. I feel a lightness in my head. There is no worry or concern to weigh me down right now

... not today.

The soft sweet sound of Rainbow sings to me: "All your past pain I will take with the promise of one thing."

"Yes, anything."

"You need to allow love into your heart. In every part of your life, breathe through your heart. Look at your husband. He loves you completely. Your own courage to embrace life will give freedom to the past that once haunted you."

It sounded easy but my own heart knows the struggle. I know the work it takes to mend being splintered, shattered and shut off. My heart was revived only a few years ago with the promise to trust. I have felt deeply and I accept that the past cannot be changed. Today, though, it seems I have a choice.

"From today, I promise to live through my heart. Can you give me a sign that when the rain stops the sky will gift a rainbow? This will show me this is possible," I ask.

"Remember to look up," Rainbow hints.

After more time exploring the family grove of

the rainbow gums, Michael and I run back to the car, dripping wet. We had packed a towel in case we went into one of the swimming holes today, so we attempt to dry off.

Heading back up the coast toward our Maui home, I tell Michael that all we need now is a rainbow in the sky.

After about 20 minutes, the rain stops completely. The sun shines from behind some clouds just before it prepares to set in the evening sky. Michael pulls the car over to watch people surfing on the beach below.

Excitedly, I leap from the car. A massive rainbow is reaching across the sky in the distance, each end disappearing into the earth. It is the sign I asked for. This means that my freedom from past pain is possible. I can do this!

I have loved rainbows since I was young. I was told the rainbow was a miracle, a promise that floods would never cover the earth again. Now as an adult I search for multitude meanings of the rainbow. Among the folklore is a Chinese legend of yin and yang coming together in perfect harmony and the balance when a rainbow hangs in the sky. A rainbow can represent the bridge into one's heart, filled with awe and love ... 'over the rainbow' and towards the pot of gold. All the beautiful colours of our chakras are in order, just like a rainbow.

It is magical and perhaps I will find my pot of gold.

CHAPTER 2

Choice

Another day has dawned. This time without rain and only mud underfoot, I carefully walk towards Rainbow. Strong yet elegant she stands, holding this beautiful space for me. Walking closer I feel her energy and the fine hairs on my arm stand on end. I cannot help but smile as I marvel at her colourful stripy bark. This time when I visit she is dry and the colours are not as vibrant.

"Morning," I say.

"I wondered when I would see you again," her melody sings out.

It has been about a week since my first visit to see Rainbow. My travel has taken me to the mainland of Hawaii to meet with friends.

"I haven't been avoiding you. I just wanted a quiet time to digest the message of our first meeting," I said honestly.

I know she already understands my struggle. In my heart she is now threaded. She knows that the idea of being completely free of my "story of brokenness" is exciting, yet leaves me fearful that my own identity will be ripped away. I have felt nervous about living with a vulnerable heart and have retracted a little from Michael this past week. Fear is preventing all my hopes and dreams of living my life full of joy.

I honestly share with Rainbow: "I've felt confusion and have distracted myself this past week. I have questioned if I am up for the task. I was excited about the promise of being completely free of past pain and hurt, but now I question if I am worthy."

"You have a stirring deep within. The growth in you will forever change the way you live. You wouldn't have met me if you weren't ready. Remember the rainbow across the sky just after we met, the sign that change is possible? You can do this!"

I am encouraged by Rainbow.

Shyly I look at the ground and move my foot in the shape of a rainbow.

"As soon as I open my heart around Michael,

his energy also changes. He mirrors my fear of the unknown," I share.

I know that when my own energy changes, everyone will respond differently around me.

"Subtle changes right now. No announcements needed. Be kind and grateful, and your heart will lead the way."

I feel relief not having to wake up to a "new" me right away. I am granted a gentle transition. This way I am sure I can continue my efforts to vanquish the fear I first felt.

"I am nervous but trust your promise to bring me joy," I respond.

"Remember to begin with self-love. When you love within, it is easier to love throughout."

At that moment I feel a final burst of love shoot right through me. Today my own gentle gift warms me.

CHAPTER 3

A Shift in Being

Returning to my life in Australia, I begin to feel a shift. I manage the dreaded long flight with ease. In the laundry sits a mound of washing. Only a couple of loads have managed to make their way through the machine during my trip.

Up early I sort, wash, hang, fold and place clean clothes onto the beds of the family I love. Usually I would complain, curse, be annoyed or get angry about others not pulling their weight, but now I feel different – I consider it a privilege to live in a home with a washer and the resources to create order. In Waikiki I saw many homeless people, rummaging through bins for a meal or a cast-off drink. Their clothes were dirty and their lives discarded. I watched on as their lives were ignored. I struggled, but they struggled more to make it through each day. I, on the other hand, live in a home. Everything is easy. Who am I to complain? I feel privileged. Load after load of washing gives me a sense of accomplishment.

I invite all the boys and their girlfriends over to dinner. This is something I have let slide for a little while, because I have felt overwhelmed by the fuss of preparing a meal that I wasn't sure would be appreciated. Tonight my focus is on spending quality time with my family. The night ends with us looking at funny photos of the boys as they grew up. Everyone laughs. We are uplifted and unified. Love is seeping back into my life in unpredictable ways.

In bed tonight, I feel my beautiful rainbow thread her magic, not only through me, but through other parts of my life also.

This evening, as my spirit takes me back to Rainbow, I feel a lightness in my step. I hear several birds singing their last chorus as the night sky is embossed with sparkly stars.

Taking my three connected breaths into my heart I feel a surge of vibrancy all around me.

"I didn't think a shift had occurred until I arrived back home. Whilst hanging clothes on my clothesline today I understood what you meant about living through my heart." I am busting to tell Rainbow about my "light bulb" moment.

"A subtle shift can create ripples in many ways. Do you find yourself more present?" Rainbow asks.

"Yes that's exactly what I feel. I usually daydream away my day and am often annoyed that I am still stuck with the same," I confess.

"Have you been worried about what others might think?" Rainbow asks.

"No, I haven't even given that a thought! You know, this way of thinking in the past took up so much of my time. I would do what was expected to receive praise. But now I haven't even cared whether anyone thanked me for doing their washing. I have gained satisfaction just by serving those I love," I say.

"Continue, you are more than ready." These are the last words spoken by Rainbow tonight.

I smile, happy that I have gained a happier way of feeling and doing life a little more easily. I am getting so much done.

"Thank you."

Holding my hand to the colours of Rainbow, I feel calm and ready for more.

CHAPTER 4

Between Opposites

I can't wait to connect with Rainbow today.

Running up the embankment, now completely dry, I head towards the mother tree at the back of the grove of rainbow gums.

"I couldn't wait to visit today," I excitedly tell Rainbow.

"Stop and catch your breath. It is great to see you so excited. Why are you in such a hurry this morning?" Rainbow tries to calm me.

"What can you tell me about the connection between light and dark? I want to know the point of difference." I know this is an open-ended question. But I am curious what my friend Rainbow can share.

"There is always a grey area where everything can shift one way or another. Blended, black and white become grey. Between happiness and sadness is complacency. Between depression and overwhelming joy is neutrality. Being in that middle space is a choice, as well as leaning in either direction."

There is a silent pause. I let the thought of extremes and the middle space become clear to me. But I feel compelled to ask, "Do you know what the magnet is that draws someone either way?"

"Imagine strings tied to a person's hands, feet, head or body. Whatever they are connected to from the past may have a stronger hold and tug on them. If there is pain then they may be dragged into a darker shade of living. If they are free from old ways of unhappiness, then the strings will naturally be drawn to a lighter, brighter way of life," Rainbow responds.

I picture a person being dragged in one direction or another, depending on the things to which she is connected. She is just a puppet.

"How can someone do this by choice?" I know that Rainbow did this for me once I chose to live life through my heart. I just want to know how someone can do this for themselves.

"Imagine events that still hold pain. See a string

to each of these. They connect with different places in your body. I want you to cut each cord connection on your body, allowing the pain of these events to vanish. Remember they can then consciously dissolve."

I can envisage this, and the eventual freedom that follows … the darkness turning to lightness, depression to joy. There is no longer sadness, but an abiding happiness.

"Can anyone do this?" I ask.

"It all starts with the decision to live life through your heart, being strong and finding courage to let go of the old story. Being ready to live a life of joy," Rainbow reminds me.

I know of my own struggle with this. I have to trust the process and allow life, rather than try to force it.

I lie down on the grass beside Rainbow. With eyes closed I focus on my body . The tugging of the past has released its hold. I am free to live, to not lean into the darkness. I am glad that to gain more understanding about what Rainbow has done within me.

Today I am free, light, happy and full of joy.

CHAPTER 5

Rainbow's Beginning

Closing my eyes in a dream-like state, I take another three long and slow breaths. Instant connection grants me permission to enter a timeless space, filled with wonder, seeing back to the beginning of Rainbow. I see the grove being dug and saplings being pushed into earth. More than eighty years before my giant tree friend stands before me I see a beginning filled with love and hard work. Then time speeds up and I watch as growth pushes her upwards toward the heavens. Year after year passes until today, when I rest, witnessing this grove of trees holding hands way beneath the earth. I can see support and community. One tree's happiness is always shared with the others.

I feel a pulse run through me as my connection now deepens.

"I never want to leave this sense of belonging

that I'm experiencing right now," I say aloud as I look way up into the many arms of Rainbow stretching far and wide.

"I embrace you, sister, with everything. You trusted not only me, but yourself. Take this feeling and share way beyond."

I have never before experienced such a sense of completeness. I hold my hands to my bursting heart, then reach out with my arms. Speechless with the tingle that runs within and spills out of every pore, I feel more alive than I could ever have imagined was possible. I soak it all in. Time is irrelevant. Endless and boundless, I feel part of a universe that flies unconstrained, like a small butterfly never stuck, always free.

I have no idea how long I sit there before I finally say, "Never before have I felt anything so magical. Thank you, from my heart."

"For trusting and giving up your old story, you can truly begin to feel free." Rainbow's soft loving voice caresses me. "Today, know that your dream of existence becomes you. Today, and every morning from now on, you will breathe in, knowing that you are never alone. You are human, yes, yet you are so much more. The world cries out for your song. When a pure, healed heart can be counted, the vibrant shades of rainbow continue to shine out. A promise of devastation is replaced with a pot of gold."

Her musical melody encourages my state of pure joy. I feel unimagined happiness and I know it is meant for more than just me. I imagine a world full of wonder, pure bliss and stillness; my smile, my heartbeat and my passion.

I say, "I've seen your beginning, your growth up until now. I'm a witness to the community of your rainbow family of love. Together, can the human world become like you?"

"It all starts with just one person. Carry the message within you to share with everyone who listens, feels and trusts self. Most importantly, it is possible for everyone to love self in the way you experience today. Imagine the world with all past pain banished from existence."

I wonder if I can continue to feel as I do right now, standing beside Rainbow. Will my own bubble float up and be pierced? I commit myself to remembering this sense of aliveness, to always breathe in, remembering whence my air first came.

"Thanking you is not enough for the gift I carry

in my heart. My gratitude for living and dreaming is enormous."

 I look towards Rainbow and see that I reflect her, and she me.

CHAPTER 6

Freedom

I think of everyone who has shared a moment with me across my life – those who said "no" and those who said "yes". I've certainly not been championed by all. Yet everyone has had a role in getting me to this point in my life. I've learned the value of forgiveness. It is never OK to be in the hands of the monster as a child. Yet today my abuser's grip has finally been released. It is never OK that someone's own self-loathing can cast a shadow onto others. This shadow was where I used to hide. I am grateful that enough people showed up in my life to bring a spark of brightness, people who believed in me. At times I haven't been able to find any belief in myself. My own fire within has been snuffed and needed re-lighting. In the end, my own self-belief is what has really mattered.

I realise that not everyone will understand me. It is not always for others to know me. To know myself as important, valuable and special far outweighs a stranger's approval. I have feared judgement and others' opinions, and now I recognise that this has kept me silent for way too long.

Today I realise that the world is better while I'm happy, really happy. This is only possible when I let those who love me, close to me. My own self-love is important, but not always easy as I have carried my story, hurt and pain. Now I make myself a promise that in giving up my own harsh history, I will never give up on myself.

I walk up to Rainbow with a single question: "I still have one thing to do this year that ties me to the past. I've forgiven, but it always makes me sad. In a courtroom, will I survive?"

"This one thread still tugs at your heart. Know when you have completed this history's chapter, that this thread will be cut and you will be free. Know that your heart's final tear will not hold you there for long. It will be complete. Freedom is already yours."

My heart bursts with fullness. My own compassion, love and understanding tell me I will be OK. I am no longer filled with fear or doubt.

CHAPTER 7

Simple Pleasures

Every little detail of my life creates a fragment to add to the bigger puzzle. Without all the details, the full picture cannot be seen.

Dressing each morning becomes an extension of how I feel. I've started to choose vibrant colours that make me feel happy. Years ago, when I opened my wardrobe doors, I could see only black. No more.

Eating only because my body is hungry is new to me. Before, food was a distraction or a tool to push down emotions stuck within. I no longer starve myself, then fill up on sugar to ferment and go rancid. My body has calmed and is now digesting life. Stiff joints inflamed by annoyance are softened with love and understanding. I had believed that by stubbornly ignoring my rheumatoid arthritis, it would eventually politely leave my body. Now I treat my joints with care, moving gently to avoid flare-ups. I satisfy my hunger with food that supports me, rather than swallowing fads or trendy ways of eating. I have worked to make all the pieces of my puzzle support me.

Visiting Rainbow, I look into the cloud-free sky above. There is a beautiful, deep, expansive blue, as far as my eyes can see.

"I cannot believe how much I've gained by being present in my life," I say.

"Your eyes are the colour of the sky today. So good to see you," Rainbow returns the greeting.

"I am so excited about life. Can you share something with me today to give me another new gift?"

"Of course, it would be my pleasure."

There is a pause, almost like Rainbow is pondering which of her many insights is most relevant right now.

"When the simplest things bring you pleasure, you will no longer search for escape. Addicts of any kind want escape from the present, their 'now' is always too tangled with their 'yesterday'. By being completely present to the details of eating, dressing, cleaning, working, talking, thinking, feeling, living and loving, you hold in your existence a profound and simple gift."

Because I've woken to mindfulness, I understand this to be true. Is there anything more?

Before I can ask, Rainbow continues:

"Manifestation is the magic of dreaming for more. When you wake each morning, ask to be inspired. Ideas will flutter into your net, ready to be grasped. Write them down and watch them grow. In the evening before you settle in bed, release all that needs to be let go. Only hold onto the dreams you have caught, and they will dance with you as you sleep."

"That's beautiful. Thank you. I will definitely catch dreams to inspire and manifest magic."

I hold my hand on the many layers of bark, each offering a different hue. My friend Rainbow is right. I need to focus on great things and discard the rest, remembering that each detail brings the full picture into view.

My friend Rainbow gently moves, as the breeze caresses her beauty. Her many branch-arms sway, as though she's beckoning me closer. Closing my eyes, I feel sunshine warming my face.

"I look at you, as you do me. I notice your limbs, as you do mine. Sun kisses your skin, as my own bark is warmed," Rainbow continues our conversation.

My heart and soul leap with joy. My view of beauty has captured me, casting its spell of happiness. I don't have to conjure up any effort – I can simply be.

"I am grateful for your gift of love and beauty," I say.

I love being in this relaxed space that holds me so tenderly.

"Perception – your view will always be reflective of you. If you are angry, you will see only shadows. If happy, it will be like the sun is shining on your scene," Rainbow adds.

"Yes, but I feel you are the one who banished my past pain, you are the one who energised my being," I say.

"Remember that I asked first if you could live through your heart. You waited, as you were afraid of giving up your story. You felt your own identity would be lost ..." Rainbow reminds me.

She is right. I avoided connecting to Rainbow for about a week because I was weighing up my choice against all I knew. It took more courage to choose happiness rather than my usual sense of annoyance and pain. I remember my confusion and old ways of being – they feel far away now, but it hasn't been so long since they shaped my life.

"So my way of happiness, today, comes from me?" I ask.

"You, my friend, had to make a decision about trust. Vulnerable 'you' had hidden and felt she needed permission to be."

"Is this a deeper gift?" I ask.

"The gift is in the choice. I can be as I am today, gently swaying in the breeze and basking in the sunshine. Others can walk up and see what their own heart reflects. Closed hearts would only see a tree. Opens heart would feel, and free spirits ready to fly would experience it all. It always comes down to a choice. Your choice has brought you back to me, to soak again and again in my love. I can see you are bursting to share this also with others," Rainbow observes.

I smile because the truth is I have questioned

this time whether I am meant to share the gift of this tree. I have wondered if I am the only one meant to see her beauty.

"I thought it was my duty to re-gift you to the world. I was told once that if a tree gives a gift, then it is never just for me," I say honestly, explaining why I've been so committed to sharing the gifts of the trees.

"Again, it is always a choice."

She is right. My own longing has to first be a decision for more. My lack of contentment had pushed me forward, reaching for something more. I've dreamed of freedom from my past. I've wanted to unlearn unhealthy patterns. I knew I could be more. For a long time, I just didn't know what to do next.

"It has been your love that has bought you joy."

I look back up towards the sky. Then I turn my gaze towards the ground. Closing my eyes I turn and lean my back against my friend. My own change has been made possible by the seed she has planted – a seed of choice. I could have discarded the idea entirely, or nurture it and let it grow.

CHAPTER 8

Held by Angel

My heart is heavy as I make my way toward Rainbow. Today marks the loss of a beautiful girl in my history. She was like a daughter to me and we should have been celebrating her birthday today. I still feel the pain of her loss.

I usually choose vibrant colour from my wardrobe, but today I wear black.

"Rainbow, today I feel sadness in memory of someone I love so much," I almost choke on my words. "I wish I could hold her one more time. I can feel her beautiful spirit, but it's just not the same."

I hang my head as tears run down my face.

"Loss is always etched into your heart in her memory. Today, hold a space for your pain. Pick a flower, light a candle or write a note. Your tears allow love to flow."

As Rainbow says this, the Maui sky opens itself to the rain once more.

"The universe mourns the loss of loved ones. Just like you, trees also feel the void. I feel the sorrow in your heart but I also feel some joy for the beautiful memories with the one you call Angel."

I have so many memories. I smile as I remember her referring to me as one of her Mums. I too looked out for her as one of my own. I held her hand when she felt pain. I gowned up for one of her medical procedures. My memories take me back to her infectious laugh. She could light up a whole room. She had loved all things vibrant. She would have loved to be here with me now, with Rainbow Gum.

I know this space is one of magic. I blink and look again. Walking toward me at Rainbow is my beautiful Angel.

"How have you brought my Angel here to me?" I ask.

"Through our spirit connection, I've invited your girl here. Take this special moment."

Angel walks towards me, wearing a beautiful, violet, flowing dress. Her blonde hair glistens in the light as the sun peeks out now from the darkened clouds. A magnificent rainbow fills the sky. My breath is taken away by her beauty and magic. Into my arms falls my Angel. I hold her in silence. Tears of joy cover my face. We look into each other's eyes, both wiping away tears. She tells me she often visits loved ones. She is no longer in pain. She asks if I can feel happiness when I feel, hear or remember her. I promise to try.

A butterfly full of Angel's essence replaces her human form. Around me, she flies and settles on my shoulder for a brief moment. This moment of holding and loving her again is a gift. I remember that she was just like the butterfly – on earth her incredible beauty was a gift for but a brief time, before she spread her own wings to fly free.

I watch as the butterfly flies away.

"Thank you for bringing Angel to me. I loved holding her and her memory. Seeing her fly filled me with joy," I thank Rainbow.

"Your spirit loved ones are never far. Remember to call them by name. Nature holds a reflection of them all, so remember to look for their signs."

The butterfly held a special symbol today and I feel abundantly grateful.

I turn and face Rainbow: "Thank you for holding space for me today, for turning my sadness into a special moment."

I hear the echo of Angel telling me she loves me. Her sweet soul floats to be with all she loves.

I rest my back against Rainbw. No more words. I feel love tingle my face. My body feels a soft heartbeat that's mine, yet somehow it is beating differently. My tone is lighter, no longer heavy.

Closing my eyes, I see darkness filled by colour, one by one. Like drops of paint they pool together in a puddle, swirling and creating patterns. My inner view is filled with love. My breathing is slow and long. I am restful.

Although I miss my Angel, I feel her love. After the rain today I saw a beautiful rainbow. The sun warms my soul. My gift is feeling and allowing.

Fly, Angel, fly.

CHAPTER 9

Love is a Gift

I have experienced many subtle changes since meeting Rainbow. My own restrictions of doubt, worry and dread – the feelings that I used to wake up with most mornings – have gently released their hold. I am grateful to Rainbow for infusing colour into the grey areas of my life.

Three breaths are barely needed as I find myself, in spirit, at the foot of Rainbow. I'm bursting with appreciation about the way my life has changed.

"Hello, Rainbow. I'm finding the gift of living life through my heart. You were right when you said that past pains would dissolve. I feel good. Thank you."

"I can see and feel your energy. I believe you are now ready."

A gust of tropical warm breeze twirls and dances with my clothing, messing up my hair. I grab my dress to prevent it blowing right up.

"Do you want me to do something?" I ask.

"Your husband Michael has flown to his mother's homeland in Holland so he can surprise her for Mother's Day. Have you thought of your own mother these past few days?"

Well, strangely I had. She hasn't filled many of my thoughts for many years. There was too much pain so I instead avoided thinking of her.

"I keep on picturing myself writing to Mum. I've thought of her a lot these past few days," I confess, still a little surprised imaging myself writing to my mother. "Am I being shown what I am meant to do?"

"You will know when you are ready and the time is right," Rainbow reassures me.

"Alright, let's see what happens."

I make no promises.

I stand in the tropics, feeling warmth in my heart. Perhaps my heart cracks are now healed and smoothing over.

"Remember just after we met, I told you to trust. Trust me, you are ready now." Rainbow is confident.

With Michael away, I am feeling a little lost. I ring a girlfriend and we catch up for pizza and fizz. I end up staying the night.

The next day we go out for breakfast. There is no break in the flow of our conversation. When driving towards the shops, I take a shortcut right past my Mum's home. I explain to my friend that this is where I grew up. I also share with her about the insistent thought of writing a note to my Mum.

At the shops, I feel drawn to act. I purchase a small gift card.

We head back to my mother's house and my friend offers to hand-deliver my message of love while I wait in the car around the corner. In a moment of complete surrender, I feel nervousness, mixed with love. Real love is a gift.

When we drive away, my friend thanks me for the privilege of delivering the note. It is only a year since her own Mum left earth.

Mother's Day this year is also the birthday of my youngest son. He is 19. I spend my day doing what I love, cooking up a storm.

Flowers, chocolates, scented room aroma and wine are my gifts from others. The gift to me is having so much love in my life.

Because of the international time difference, I stay up late to watch the surprise captured by Michael, seeing his parents. His Mum nearly jumps out of her skin when she realises that Michael is with them in Amsterdam!

I feel content as I put away the last dish and hang out the washing before I head to bed. Sleep tonight takes a little while, because I am awake. I have woken to a new way of "me".

CHAPTER 10

I Am

I've started receiving comments that I look and sound different. I'm told I look really happy. I always reply that I am.

My heart way of living definitely has vanquished a lifetime of hurt and pain. I feel that that which once dragged me down like a vortex of darkness, has released its hold. Instead of being held back, I feel encouraged to move forward.

Sitting at the base of Rainbow, I enquire: "I would love to know your name."

"My name is Kiama, which means magic."

"The magic of you, my friend, has been such an incredible gift. Kiama is a beautiful name," I respond.

"My name, just like yours, was a gift from someone else. At your birth and as my own sapling grew, I was given my name."

My own vision takes me back to my own beginning. I see my own mother's arms, cradling a tiny, fragile baby – me. Fed, clothed and held. I feel love. This was a time before life's harsh impressions changed me, a time before I was being dragged, hurt and changed.

Then I am taken to all the times of darkness in my life. I sense the feeling of love before the darkness began. Then I witness all the events through my life that changed me, that shrouded me with shadows.

Finally, I witness pure love. Love has come into my world, changing each life event of darkness. I return to the purity I was born to embrace.

As I rest my back against Kiama Rainbow, she gently says, "You have woken to the love that first held you. Your pain today is completely released, because you trusted and could remain in your heart, living your life this new way. You can speak your story without having to relive it. Speak the truth of you. Be proud of receiving your true essence once more."

My life does feel present. I am experiencing more gratitude. My life is not a right, but a privilege.

"Thank you."

I take three breaths into my heart. Then, instead of connecting into my friend Rainbow, I connect completely into myself.

Without a doubt, the gift of Rainbow is living my life through my heart, without my mind getting in the way. She is the tree of "Joy". Before this I never really knew what it was like to feel this way constantly. I experienced snippets of this, but they were never sustained enough to let me notice the details of my life. Now when someone speaks, I listen and hear without my own chatter distracting me. I look into the eyes of my loved ones and see their beauty as a reflection of my own. My life is lived in spontaneity and realness.

"You see my truth, my gifts and my heart," Rainbow says.

"I see you as you reflect me. Becoming my mirror, I can see what I craved. Now I am all that I dream."

I felt happy and know that this is reflective of how Rainbow feels.

"One last thing before you turn and walk away. It's time to stop shying away from your beauty and gifts. You are the difference that the world craves.

Be strong, stand proud – and be you," Rainbow tells me.

I understand what she means. For so long I have been hiding, fearful of judgement, not only from others but also my own inner critic. Finally I'm ready to be me and I know that this is my unique treasure, my own gift that I now freely give myself. I give permission to show up, speak, express and accept. I feel a confidence I've never felt before, as well as a softness. My barrier has been removed.

My hope and dream is for this feeling to be felt by everyone. I imagine my own self-love stretching like a ripple across the sky, reaching everyone – perhaps just like a rainbow.

I am, you are, we are all here to be set free.

CHAPTER 11

Happy Birthday

Today marks a milestone in my life. I know it is important to re-visit my beautiful sister Rainbow. Kiama is such a big part of my life. I want to connect to her joy and my own in return.

Walking up the embankment, I follow the path to the back of Rainbow's grove family and I instantly feel an electric buzz that lifts my spirit.

"Good morning Kiama, my rainbow sister."

I walk a full circle around before I sit with my back resting against her magic.

"Happy birthday, Rochelle."

I want to ask how she knows, and then remember our threading. Her heart is seeded in mine, as mine is in hers.

"Meeting you just before my 50th birthday in Maui

is one of my favourite gifts." I beam with happiness. "I have organised something so special that I want to share with you. I have asked for the people who are special in my life to gift me with a small bead. I'm going to take all these beads and thread them into a necklace of love."

I am already receiving these treasures and my heart is bursting with all the dear people in my life who have gone to an effort with love to be part of this.

"Rainbow, can you tell me how trees show their family and other loved trees their love?" I am curious.

"Energy, of love, is the elixir of life. Starved of love, all those who live eventually die a slow death. Trees are no different, you know. My grove is my family. Through the air, we send each other love. Through the ground, our roots send not only love but nutrients to each another as well. If a tree is sick, we all send love. When a tree dies, we all mourn its loss. The energy of sadness sweeps a forest floor when loss is felt."

This isn't something I've really put much thought into. I imagine the pain felt as large purpose-built plantations were planted, with the intention of one day being cut down. I think of all the wood used globally. My memory takes me to the palms cut down in Borneo, to how it felt while I was there. There was a vast empty space, and even the orangutans were misplaced. My heart felt heavy.

"I feel sad about what happens to tree families worldwide. Here in Maui Hawaii, do you feel the trees in other parts of the world?"

"Yes, we do. Just as you have the internet as a web to connect you, we are connected by our underground root systems. We feel and send messages, energy and love. The Rainbow Gums bring joy to all."

I imagine the buzz I feel sitting at the base of Rainbow being felt globally. I smile.

Today my own family will be sharing time, space and love together. For my birthday, we have travelled to the top of Australia, into the rainforests of the Daintree. I imagine the magical effect that this tropical wonder will have on us just in our visit.

"Rainbow, you have given me many gifts. Joy has been my most treasured. You have shared your essence, your wisdom with me, and dissolved my pain and hurt. Knowing that new sorrows can be honoured and released by living through my heart is a powerful gift. Thank you for showing me how to do all this."

"Birthday blessings, Rochelle. Remember to continue to connect to yourself always, by breathing into your heart. Look, feel, listen, experience, breathe and be present to your life right now. Collect the precious moments when loved ones connect with you through actions, words or kindness. I love your tangible threading of the precious beads from loved ones. I will always send you my love. Please place my essence, the oil you made onto three wooden beads and know that I am part of your necklace too."

"This I will definitely do. Thank you. From my heart to yours, thank you."

My 50th birthday is spent with my four sons and loving husband.

They gift me with a spa treatment while they go and play golf.

The next day we drive and walk the Daintree. We all feel the magic of time spent together in nature.

I will treasure the moments of being still, remembering to listen to the beat of my own heart.

Within this space, I have finally discovered joy.

Also by Rochelle

Banyan Tree Wisdom: My Gift to You

Banyan Tree Wisdom: Wisdom Cards

Meeting Rosie Banyan:
Learning Forgiveness, Trust and Love

I Give You My Word: Journal

EARTH GIANT TREE GIFT SERIES (GIFT BOOKS & AUDIO BOOKS)

Book 1: Oak Tree's Gift

Book 2: Baobab Tree's Gift

Book 3: Banyan Tree's Gift

Book 4: Rainbow Gum's Gift

ALCHEMY OILS

Banyan Tree: 'Restore Balance', 'Dream',
'Release' & 'Beauty Wisdom Power'

Oak Tree: 'Truth'

Baobab Tree 'Connection'

Banyan Tree 'Balance'

Rainbow Gum 'Joy'

www.treevoice.global

About the Author

A busy business owner, wife and mother, Rochelle thrived in the corporate and finance world in her early adult years. Then, after her fourth son, a wave of post-natal depression debilitated her, forcing her to re-visit the horrors of her sexually abusive childhood. With grit and determination she laboured against her own broken past and breathed life back into her shutdown heart, cracking open its language and capturing it in writing. She learned to trust in the universal soul path she'd stepped onto.

Each time she experienced a healing method that helped her, Rochelle became qualified in that field to then help others. She became a Bowen Therapist, Reiki and Seichem Master, Clinical Hypnotherapist using NLP methods, Journey Worker and Intuitive Healer. She also owned and ran a Day Spa and Healing Centre in North East Victoria.

Rochelle now immerses herself in connections with nature as they flow, bringing to life the lessons and messages through writing, speaking and facilitating. Her journey has led her to many parts of the globe. She has pitched to Hollywood in New York; she has hosted women's retreats in Bali; she has learned from poverty-stricken leaders in Senegal Africa; and she discovered the 'simple' life in Vanuatu.

Rochelle's message is honest, raw and authentic, and her words are greatly needed as we all navigate our next chapter here on earth.

AUTHOR, SPEAKER, ALCHEMIST, A LOVER OF NATURE AND VIBRANT LIVING

Connect with Rochelle

hello@treevoice.global

business.facebook.com/TreeVoiceAuthor

www.facebook.com/RochelleHeverenAuthor

Instagram: @rochelle_with_love_x

www.treevoice.global

www.ingramcontent.com/pod-product-compliance
Lightning Source LLC
Chambersburg PA
CBHW032052290426
44110CB00012B/1050